PERFECT
ABSTRACTION

PERFECT ABSTRACTION

BY
ADI DA SAMRAJ

NEW ESSAYS WRITTEN FOR
Transcendental Realism
The Image-Art of egoless
Coincidence With Reality Itself,
ON THE OCCASION OF ADI DA SAMRAJ'S
EXHIBITION AT THE CENACOLO DI OGNISSANTI,
FLORENCE, 2008

THE DAWN HORSE PRESS
MIDDLETOWN, CALIFORNIA

Copyright © 2008 The Avataric Samrajya of Adidam Pty Ltd,
as trustee for The Avataric Samrajya of Adidam.
All rights reserved.

No part of this book may be copied or reproduced in any manner
without written permission from the publisher.
(The Dawn Horse Press, 10336 Loch Lomond Road, #305, Middletown, California 95461, USA)

The Avataric Samrajya of Adidam Pty Ltd, as trustee for The Avataric Samrajya of Adidam,
claims perpetual copyright to this book, to the entire Written (and otherwise recorded)
Reality-Teaching of Avatar Adi Da Samraj, to the Image-Art of Adi Da Samraj,
and to all other writings, recordings, and images it owns.

Produced by the Dawn Horse Press,
a division of the Avataric Pan-Communion of Adidam.

International Standard Book Number: 978-1-57097-250-8

CONTENTS

THE COVER IMAGES 7

INTRODUCTION 9

PERFECT ABSTRACTION
BY
ADI DA SAMRAJ

New Essays Written for
Transcendental Realism
The Image-Art of egoless Coincidence With Reality Itself

I. The Maze of Ecstasy 13

II. The Self-Discipline of Ecstatic Participation 27
In The Image-Art I Make and Do

III. Open-Handed Image-Art 33

IV. Perfect Abstraction 35

GLOSSARY 39

The Order of The Day: Saturday 15
(from *Geome One: Alberti's Window*)

He-and-She Is Me (The Indivisible Singleness of Reality Itself): Part Four / 5
(from *Geome Four: The Subject In Question*)

THE COVER IMAGES

Adi Da Samraj creates his image-art not as isolated works, but as suites of closely related images. A single suite may comprise as many as several hundred individual works of image-art.

At the exhibition *Transcendental Realism: The Art of Adi Da Samraj*—in Florence, at the Cenacolo di Ognissanti, from February 23 through June 22, 2008, as part of *Inverno a Firenze*—four monumental images by Adi Da Samraj are on display. Each of these images comes from a different suite.

For the cover and back cover of *Perfect Abstraction*, images have been chosen which represent two of the suites on view in Florence—*Geome One: Alberti's Window* and *Geome Four: The Subject In Question*.

The largest works from *Geome One* are (like the work on view in Florence) very long monumental images, each composed of seven seamless panels. Each of the panels is named for a day of the week (Sunday through Saturday). Within the suite as a whole, each "day" exists in many different visual forms. The image on the cover of *Perfect Abstraction* is the fifteenth of a group of thirty-two forms of "Saturday".

In *Geome One: Alberti's Window*, Adi Da "reverses" Leon Battista Alberti's paradigm of "painting as window". Rather than creating an illusion of perspective—an illusion that ultimately points back to the viewer (thereby reinforcing self-identity)—the images of *Alberti's Window* invite the viewer to relinquish self-identity by entering into a world free of perspective.

Like many of Adi Da's suites, *Geome Four: The Subject In Question* includes not only images in color but also images that are purely in black-and-white. While the image on view

7

in Florence is a complex composition of colored geometric fields, the image on the back cover of *Perfect Abstraction* is a similarly complex composition of linear forms—with both black lines on a white field and white lines on a black field. In Adi Da's description, the highly intricate structure of the imagery in *Geome Four* "puts the perceiver in touch with how experience is organized by mind, brain, and body", drawing the viewer "into a root-level of experience". The geometric forms become building blocks of superstructures pointing to the non-duality of existence. ∎

NOTE: The works from *Geome One* and *Geome Four* which are displayed at the Florence exhibition are reproduced in *Transcendental Realism: The Art of Adi Da Samraj* (Middletown, Calif.: Da Plastique, 2007). Please see page 48.

INTRODUCTION

This collection of essays comprises additions by Adi Da Samraj to his book *Transcendental Realism* since the publication of *Aesthetic Ecstasy* in August/September 2007. Thus, this booklet is intended to add to and accompany both of those texts.

The essays in *Perfect Abstraction* present a wide range of commentary by Adi Da Samraj on his image-art and the process he engages to create images. The title of this booklet points to the unique "method" whereby Adi Da Samraj creates images that are a means of access to the Reality that is Prior even to perception. Altogether, these essays describe the kind of "dance" Adi Da Samraj engages to develop free images that transcend, rather than merely play upon, the apparent "subject-and-object" context of visual art. ∎

PERFECT ABSTRACTION
BY
ADI DA SAMRAJ

NEW ESSAYS WRITTEN FOR
Transcendental Realism
The Image-Art of egoless
Coincidence With Reality Itself

The Maze of Ecstasy

1.

During the Renaissance, perspective—or the systematic and "scientifically" rule-based representation of physically-perceived, or, otherwise, mentally-conceived, "subjects" as if they are being observed by a spatially and temporally "point-of-view-located" viewer—became the fixed and idealized basis of Western image-art. When an artistic image is created on the basis of the rules (and the ego-affirming idealism) of perspective, everything in the image points (or refers back) to the viewer—or the "point of view" of ego. Thus, beginning with the Renaissance, "point of view" (itself), or ego (itself), became the root-"subject" and fixed ideal of Western image-art and of the totality of Western culture.

It is an irony that the Western Renaissance—or the historical period that saw the formulation of Copernican cosmology, which asserted the centrality of the Sun, rather than of the Earth—is also the historical period of the assertion of the centrality of Man (and of the egoic individual), rather than any presumption of the Divine, as the essential "subject" of human "knowledge", culture, and history. The Western Renaissance was the birth of human ego-culture—and perspectivally-constructed image-art was a fundamental device and sign of that ego-culture and its idealization of the individuality of "point of view".

Perspectival image-art originated with the analysis of how things appear from the "point of view" of an individual human observer. On the basis of that analysis, the artists of the early Renaissance developed a systematic and mathematically precise method of rendering a painted image as it would otherwise be constructed by the eye of the individual observer. However, it is not merely the physical eye that constructs the perspectival view of the world. Most fundamentally, it is "point of view" (itself), or ego (itself), that constructs the perspectival view. Thus, perspectival imagery represents what ego (or "point of view") makes of the world.

In the conventions of perspectival image-art, the physical eye and the ego-"I" are the same.

The intrinsically ego-transcending root-presumption associated with the image-art I make and do is precisely the opposite of the ego-based and ego-idealizing root-presumption associated with perspectival image-art. Perspectival image-art glorifies the ego's construction of the world—as if that ego-constructed world is (itself) Reality Itself—whereas Reality Itself is always Prior to the ego's construction of a world and Prior to any and every "point of view" within the world.

The world that the ego—or any spatial and/or temporal "point of view"—sees is not how Reality Itself Is. My image-art is based on an aesthetic that is rooted in how Reality Itself Is. My image-art always undermines the "position" of the ego, or the will of the ego to feel that it is "located" in a world of its own construction.

Therefore, the image-art I make and do does not point to—or idealize, and depend upon, and assert the position and the separateness of—the viewer. Indeed, the image-art I make and do is intended to directly counter "point of view", or ego. Thus, the image-art I make and do is both aperspectival and anegoic (or non-egoic). The image-art I make and do is specifically intended to counter the ego's expectation of being able to construct a world.

2.

The advent of perspective in the early Renaissance signalled a profound paradigm shift in European civilization—a shift from a culture centered on the "God"-idea to a culture centered on the human individual, or the ego. In the Middle Ages (and earlier, even back into ancient times), the fundamental "subject" of Western art was the "idea of the Divine"—whereas, beginning with the Renaissance, and lasting until the beginning of the "modernist" period, the fundamental "subject" of Western art was the "idea of the human individual", as conveyed (in particular) by the technical device of perspective. Thus, pre-Renaissance culture was, at root, about surrendering the ego to the "God"-idea, while Renaissance culture was, at root, about the idea of magnifying the knowledge and the power of the ego, and about controlling and exploiting the world as constructed by the ego.

The various modes of avant-garde image-art in the "modernist" period arose out of—and, to a greater or lesser degree, in reaction to—the Western tradition of perspectival image-art. Arising out of this background, "modernist" avant-garde image-art played on the notion of "point-of-view"-perception—investigating various different modes of making image-art in an apparently non-perspectival manner, modes that were intended to (in one or another manner) break free of "point of view", but, nevertheless, always preserving "point of view" itself as the core "subject". The "modernist" project of achieving liberation from "point of view" (and liberation from the perception of the world constructed by "point of view") never came to a full resolution. Certain core issues remained to be dealt with. Those issues had to do, principally, with how to make art that transcends "point of view" absolutely—rather than only partially, or only by the effort of irony and seeming.

The image-art I make and do is the intrinsically ego-transcending (and, thus and thereby, perspective-transcending, or intrinsically aperspectival) image-art that participates in (or egolessly coincides with) Reality Itself.

The image-art I make and do—rather than re-asserting myth-based ideas relative to the Divine (as in the case of pre-Renaissance image-art), or indulging in ego-based glorification of the individual "self" (as in the case of Renaissance-based pre-"modernist" image-art), or, otherwise, merely playing upon the failure of perspectivally-based ego-culture (as in the case of both "modernist" and "postmodernist" image-art)—asserts the intrinsic freedom of intrinsically ego-transcending participation in Reality Itself.

The image-art I make and do directly addresses and (thoroughly and, at last, completely) resolves <u>all</u> issues inherent in the consideration of <u>absolutely</u> transcending "point of view".

The image-art I make and do is not an art (in the pre-Renaissance manner) of picturing a "God"-idea, or of rendering some kind of visual equivalent of conventional "religion". The image-art I make and do is not an art (in the Renaissance manner) about the ego-"I", or about the methods whereby the ego-"I" constructs its version of the world. The image-art I make and do is Transcendental Realism—or the image-art of egoless coincidence with Reality Itself.

3.

There is "God-art", there is "ego-art", and there is "Reality-art".

Pre-Renaissance image-art is "God-art"—or image-art made and done relative to Deity, or deities, or gods and goddesses. Thus, pre-Renaissance image-art is about what the space-time-bound ego presumes to exist above and beyond itself. Therefore, the total image-art tradition of the pre-Renaissance West (extending back into ancient pre-Christian times) is "mythology-art"—principally intended to visually portray the mythology of divinity in one mode or another, including (in later centuries) the Christian mode. Renaissance image-art and post-Renaissance image-art (up to the "modern" period) is "ego-art"—or image-art specifically designed to portray the ego's view (or "point-of-view"-construction) of "reality", by means of the systematic application of the codified laws of perspective. Even the thoroughly secularized avant-garde Western image-art of the "modern" and "post-modern" era is still a play upon (or a failed effort to escape from) the tradition of "ego-art", or "point-of-view"-art.

The image-art I make and do is "Reality-art"—not in the conventional sense of image-art that imitates or merely reproduces ordinary "reality" (which conventional "reality-art" is another form of "ego-art"), but in the sense of image-art that <u>intrinsically</u> egolessly coincides with Reality Itself. Thus, the image-art I make and do is not about myth-based views of Reality, nor is the image-art I make and do about the ego that invents myth-based views of Reality. The image-art I make and do is about Reality <u>Itself</u>—beyond myth, and beyond egoity.

The image-art I make and do has required profound philosophical and Spiritual preparation even to be made—decades of intensive consideration regarding fundamental issues of Truth, of Reality Itself, of the means to go through and beyond all traditional and ego-based modes of thinking and understanding, in order to come to the point where I could make and do image-art on an intrinsically and entirely "point-of-view"-less basis.

4.

I remember going to a particular place at Coney Island* when I was a boy. There was a maze of multi-colored posts into which one would enter, walk around, and keep walking

---

*Coney Island was a groundbreaking resort and amusement park area in New York City, which flourished between the late 1880s and World War II.

into dead-ends. In this particular case, there were not only dead-end walls as one would walk around inside this cage of mazes, but there were also mirrors reflecting one as one walked into them, or else reflecting something obliquely, so that one lost one's sense of the space. One would constantly slam into oneself, into one's misunderstanding of the space one was in.

The nature of egoic experience is something like that. It is a maze of misunderstanding of the nature of where one is. One is constantly slamming into oneself, because one does not understand the nature of the space (or the "room") itself.

The apparent world and the ego-"I", or (space-time-"located") "point of view" that knows the world of views, are mere conventions of human design. The conventionally apparent universe is a "room" without an exit—an unending maze of shapes and signs defined and limited by the any and every "point of view" that perceives "it". Therefore, the "maze" of universe apparent to ego's "I" cannot be escaped.

All seeking is an egoically-driven effort toward the illusion of escape—either by distraction or by purification or by final fulfillment or by flight to absence. The maze of ego-"I" and the universe of endless and futile seeking cannot be escaped by any means—but the ego-"I" itself, and all of its views of universal "room", can be intrinsically (and, thus, Perfectly) transcended.

Not space-time re-"location", but ecstasy—or the intrinsic transcending of "point of view" and all space-time-"locatedness"—is the only true and possible release from the "maze of room" that is all present bondage to thought and perception. Therefore, the image-art I make and do is made and done to serve true ecstasy by aesthetic means—and, thus, by un-confining every viewer from the shape and place of "point of view".

The images of perspectival art are not merely representations of what is in the world. In perspectival image-art,

The Maze of Ecstasy

one is constantly slamming into oneself. The perspectival image—and "point-of-view"-based perception itself—is a kind of maze, in which one does not get the direct (and liberating) sighting of the Reality one is actually in. Rather than seeing Reality Itself, one is always seeing the "point-of-view"-based "reality" one has naively constructed. Therefore, one is constantly getting lost and confused. And, <u>always</u>—no matter how many landscapes, portraits, still lifes, or visual narratives one looks at—<u>all</u> perspectivally-constructed images are essentially about oneself (or the "point-of-view"-bound and space-time-bound perceiving and thinking ego-"I").

When one looks at perspectivally-based image-art, one is constantly being reminded of oneself, constantly being re-"located" in one's own position of presumed separateness. One is, in effect, constantly walking into one's own face. Thus, perspectivally-based image-art is inherently Narcissistic art—regardless of its apparent "subject" matter. Perspectivally-based image-art is, fundamentally, about the egoic "self", or separate (space-time-"located") "point of view". Thus, when viewing perspectivally-based image-art, one is constantly getting lost in a maze of mirrors and fractions, in which one cannot "locate" and understand Reality Itself.

In order to intrinsically "locate" and understand Reality Itself, the maze of "point-of-view"-based perspectival experience must be seen as a whole—or from a "position" Prior to the totality—rather than seen from "inside" (or as a partial view, and as a "point-of-view-located" separateness, trapped within the maze itself).

The image-art I make and do is about intrinsically transcending the maze of ego-based experience by standing "outside" the maze (or by standing in the <u>ecstatic</u> "position", Prior to "point of view"). The image-art I make and do is about not only showing Reality <u>As</u> It <u>Is</u>, but about using the device of images to confound the ego's effort to construct the world and to understand the world in its own image.

PERFECT ABSTRACTION

Through that confounding, the image-art I make and do serves the feelingly-participating viewer in an ecstatic and tacit understanding of Reality Itself, through the viewing of image-art that does not point to "point of view".

I have (over many decades) made all kinds of images, and the various kinds of images each have different purposes. Some of the images I have made and done are apparently in the mode, at least to some degree, of a perspectivally-based representational form of imagery. In this essay, I am summarizing the ultimate nature of all the image-art I have made and done—and, especially, the fully and finally resolved image-art to which the entire process has led.

In all the forms of image-art I have made and done, I have been engaged in a process ultimately leading to imagery that is thoroughly aperspectival and anegoic—or "point-of-view"-transcending in the fullest terms.

5.

Art is always coincident with culture, and culture is invariably bound to tradition—to all the limitations and (otherwise) all the virtues of humankind altogether. A global transformation is now required in human culture—after the devastation, or collapse, of ego-civilization in the twentieth century. Something entirely new is required—something comprehensively right.

My entire life has been spent in working to establish the basis for a "radically" new and "radically" comprehensive culture. My image-art is a summation, in artistic terms, of all the work I have done. Similarly, the books I have written are a summation, in literary and philosophical terms, of that same lifetime work. My lifetime of work has always been about the rightening of human existence and the transcending of what is binding human beings and leading them on a destructive course.

Therefore, the images I make and do—like the books I have written—are intended to establish a new paradigm of human civilization. The images I make and do are about an entirely different—and altogether ego-transcending—mode, not only of picture-making, but of living and understanding. What is now required is an epochal change in the history of human endeavor. Just as the Renaissance represented a profound summation of transformation in human endeavor, so now a new kind of transformation is happening.

The "modernists" were moving toward this transformation, but they were also making images in the midst of the virtual collapse of world-civilization in the twentieth century. Since that collapse, it is no longer possible to return to a tradition that idealizes the human ego. Indeed, what happened in the twentieth century was the definitive failure of Renaissance-originated civilization, which civilization was based on the idealization and glorification of the ego and on the wholesale adoption of the ego's perspectival view of "reality".

The Renaissance was the collapse of the "God"-civilization that preceded it—the civilization based on mythologized presumptions of what is traditionally conceived to be spatially and temporally "behind" and "above" the world. The Renaissance destroyed that earlier form of civilization. With the Renaissance, "God"-myth-based civilization was replaced with human-based civilization, or ego-civilization—or the civilization based on the myth of the human ego-"I". That ego-civilization came to its essential end in the twentieth century.

In this post-ego-civilization era, the only right basis for human existence—now, and into the future—is the establishment of a civilization that is no longer based on idealization of the ego, but also no longer based on "God"-mythologies. True and right life is neither "God"-myth-based nor ego-based. True and right life is intrinsically ego-<u>transcending</u>.

True and right life is the life of intrinsically egoless coincidence with Reality Itself. True and right life intrinsically transcends <u>all</u> mythologies—whether of "God" or of "Man".

The old civilization is ego-based and ego-bound. The old civilization idealized the ego, and it ended with a world of egos destroying one another. That course, in fact, is still happening, and must be stopped—but it cannot be stopped merely by force. A transformation of human understanding and of human processes altogether must occur—on every level, including the artistic level.

6.

When I was doing photographically-based image-art, I was dealing with the fundamental limitations in what has been (and still is, in some shadowy form) governing humankind. I did this by working to transcend the inherent limitations in the "point-of-view"-technology that is materialized as the instrument of the camera. The entire Western tradition of perspectival and ego-based image-art is enshrined in the technology of the camera. The camera is the materialization of "point of view". Thus, the camera is a device that summarizes the ego-based (and, thus, space-time-"point-of-view"-based) civilization of the last six hundred years.

I no longer work specifically with the camera, except to use it occasionally as a kind of sketchbook. Having accomplished what I needed to accomplish in camera-based work, I have now developed a mode of image-process that does not require the camera as a principal means of producing images. However, the images that I am making and doing now are aesthetic modes that came about through the ordeal of working with the "ego-technology" of the camera.

If one rightly approaches the image-art I make and do, the "point of view" (and, thus, all of ego-"I") is confounded. The image-art I make and do is not merely about some kind of punishing of the ego, or some kind of arbitrary frustrating of the viewer—as if the mere sensation of frustration were the purpose of the image-art. Rather, the image-art I make and do is purposed to serve the viewer's transcending of space-time-bondage and "point-of-view"-fixedness (and, thus, egoity itself) altogether—such that he or she can directly tacitly (and by means of aesthetic ecstasy) participate in Reality Itself.

I am not looking to represent ego in some form through the image-art I make and do, or to represent a world of a spatial configuration that ego can comprehend and feel comfortable—or even uncomfortable—with. The image-art I make and do is not a construct made by ego for the ego's purposes.

I have written at length about the image-art I make and do—in order to give fundamental guidance relative to rightly participating in the images and rightly understanding what that right participation is about. Otherwise, there will be an inevitable tendency to view the image-art I make and do in accordance with the prevailing conventions of interpreting art in the "post-modern" world—and such interpretations will inevitably tend to be misinterpretations.

The fully resolved image-art I make and do is a means to directly participate in Reality Itself—and not (in Alberti's language*) a "window" through which to view the ego's "point-of-view"-based construction of the world of conventional "reality". The fully resolved image-art I make and do is not about looking through something to something else. Likewise, the fully resolved image-art I make and do is not about looking from a "point of view" into a world constructed by "point of view" (or by perspectival and, altogether, space-time-bound perception). The fully resolved image-art I make and do has nothing to do with "point of view". The fully

---

* Leon Battista Alberti (1404–1472) was, among other things, a Renaissance artist who is known in art historical terms for his view (crucial to the development of perspective during the Renaissance) that the painter's canvas is to function as a "window" to the natural, objective world.

resolved image-art I make and do does not illustrate anything, and it does not merely reflect the natural characteristics of perception.

Altogether, there is a profound—and even absolute—difference between perspectival image-art and the fully resolved image-art I make and do.

7.

The great process of Reality Itself, the great process of human sanity, is an in-depth process. That process takes place in the depth-domain of awareness, not in the superficial domain of outer awareness. Reality Itself is the in-depth domain that intrinsically transcends ego and "point of view".

"Post-modern" civilization is secular, superficial, materialistic, outward-directed, and "object"-oriented. "Post-modern" civilization is founded on a mode of propaganda about the nature of existence that has driven humankind to the point of self-destruction. The propaganda of scientific materialism is based on the mythology of the ego, the mythology of "point of view". The perspectival method in art is an extension of egoity, a manifestation of the notion that Reality is the appearance that the ego constructs—and scientific materialism is an expression of that same presumption.

The only "reality" scientific materialism is looking at is a construct of egoity, or (space-time-"located") "point of view". Scientific materialism is looking at the "room" seen from a "point of view"—not the "room" as it Always Already Is, inclusive of all possible "points of view" and (thereby) transcending "point of view" itself.

The notion that Reality is reducible to what the ego constructs is inherently "self"-deluded and (at least potentially) insane. The image-art I make and do is made and done in order to serve the transcending of that egoically "self"-deluded (or "point-of-view"-insane) notion. Therefore, right participation in the images I make and do is, necessarily, in-depth, and not superficial.

Right participation in the images I make and do requires one to relinquish—or ecstatically feel beyond—"point of view". The images I make and do are for the purpose of serving the ecstatic transcending of "point of view"—or the intrinsic transcending of the ego-"I"-method, which is the activity of perceiving and, in effect, constructing the world from one's own separate (space-time-"located") "point of view". The images I make and do are images of the "room" (or the world, or Reality Itself) As it Is—or As the "room" itself, and not the "room" as it appears to be from any particular position within it.

Reality Itself requires the surrender and the transcending of all limitations, all "points of view"—in every one's case. Reality Itself cannot be controlled by the ego. Thus, image-art that can be controlled, contained, or comprehended from the perspective of ego (or "point of view") is a convention of egoity itself—and such image-art is, inevitably, a superficial "object" of human diversion.

What is profoundly in-depth is intrinsically egoless. What is profoundly in-depth is not what is merely "inward"—or "inside" the ego. What is profoundly in-depth is not wandering among the ego's "objects". Rather, what is profoundly in-depth is at the true root-depth—altogether Prior to ego-"I", space-time-"locatedness", and "point of view".

At the true root-depth, or the always Prior depth, there is always already no ego. That always Prior depth does not merely perceive through the eye. That always Prior depth ecstatically apprehends the Reality-Nature of the "room" itself—or the world, or Reality Itself, As It Really Is.

The intrinsic ecstasy of Prior and Perfect Depth is the root-basis for a new philosophy and a new way of life—the philosophy, the way of life, and, indeed, the necessary new global human civilization of egoless participation in Reality Itself.

The Self-Discipline of Ecstatic Participation In The Image-Art I Make and Do

1.

I make images by means of a process of abstraction.

That process of abstraction occurs in two stages.

The first stage is a process of abstraction relative to the totality of the "subject".

That first-stage process of abstraction takes place in feeling-response to the "<u>subject</u>" (with all the dimensions of meaning-force that are inherent in the "subject", whatever they may be in any particular case).

The second stage is a process of abstraction relative to the newly-created abstract image itself.

That second-stage process of abstraction takes place in feeling-response to the <u>image</u> (as a purely abstract visual form, within its own domain of visual elements).

First, there is the responsive abstracting of the "subject"—then, there is the responsive abstracting from or within the abstract image-form itself.

2.

On the one hand, the second-stage abstraction always has encoded within it all the responsiveness to the original "subject"—but, on the other hand, that second-stage process, more and more, goes ecstatically beyond any explicit visual references to the original "subject".

Ultimately, the second-stage process of abstraction goes utterly beyond all referentiality.

The image then becomes its own abstract field (or domain), containing no references beyond itself.

The image is then purely itself.

3.

To rightly view such an image is to participate in the domain of the image itself.

There are all kinds of meanings encoded in any such image—and anyone who seriously gives himself or herself over to feeling-participation in the image can enter into those meaning-dimensions.

Such feeling-participation is a performance-assisted "subjective" process.

Thus, the depth of the process depends on how profoundly the individual viewer enters into it.

4.

To view one of the second-stage abstractions most profoundly is to enter into the Transcendental Realist Field of the Domain of Reality Itself.

Every image I make and do is a means for serving the viewer's ego-transcending participation in Reality Itself.

The means is simply the image itself—not the image as referring to something else.

Ultimately, the "subject" of any image I make and do is Reality Itself.

True participation in Reality Itself is, necessarily, egoless.

Therefore, true participation in Reality Itself must transcend "point of view".

5.

When I achieve the final resolution of an image, taking into account all of its formal elements, then the process of abstraction has achieved a full and complete resolution. Then the image exists in its free final form.

6.

To examine the any image I make and do with the intention of seeing what can be said in reference to the presumed "subject" of the image is a secondary process.

That process of examination has its own legitimate interest, of course—but that process of examination is not the fundamental process of truly participating in the any image I make and do.

Ultimately, the true force of the any image I make and do is not a matter of its reference to a "subject".

Rather, the any image I make and do is, primarily, a means of participating in Reality Itself.

7.

It does not make any ultimate difference what "subject" I was originally responding to when I created any image.

Fundamentally, the any image I make and do simply exists as itself, in its own domain.

The any image I make and do has nothing directly to do with the "subject" to which I was originally responding.

The any image I make and do is never an "illustration" of the "subject" to which I was originally responding.

8.

In the any image I make and do, there are references to the "subject", and there are meaning-dimensions that relate (directly or indirectly) to the "subject"—and all such references and meanings are part of the associative mind (or psychic field) of anyone who fully participates in the image.

The responses of the viewer's associative mind (or psychic field) can be supplemented by considering (or even studying) the "subject" to which I was originally responding in making any particular image.

My own response to the "subject" is always in evidence in any particular image, and so there is always something that can be examined or said about all of that.

Every image I make and do always has its own particular aesthetic characteristics—based on meaning-response to the "subject", and (otherwise) based on the process of working with the formal elements of line, form, color, shape, and comprehensively indivisible structure.

However, true participation in the image is, fundamentally, a process of aesthetic ecstasy, a process of transcending egoity.

9.

The process of truly participating in the any image I make and do is without reference to a "subject" perceived from "point of view".

Thus, the process of truly participating in the any image I make and do is, most fundamentally, with reference to Reality Itself—Which Intrinsically Transcends "point of view".

Ultimately, the process of rightly viewing the any image I make and do is a process of forgetting "self", feeling beyond spatial and temporal "point of view", and (on that basis) freely and egolessly participating in That Which Is Prior to "point of view".

The Self-Discipline of Ecstatic Participation In The Image-Art I Make and Do

10.

There are two dimensions to Reality—the conditional, and the Non-conditional.

The image-art I make and do exhibits the two dimensions of Reality—and both of the dimensions of Reality are exhibited in the case of each and every image I make and do.

The two principal conditional aspects of the image-art I make and do are the perceived "subject" of the any image and the "point-of-view"-perceiver who looks at the image.

Reality Itself—or That Which Always Already Exists Prior to "point of view"—is the Non-conditional dimension of the image-art I make and do.

The viewer's right participation in the any image I make and do is not merely a matter of focusing "in" the any image for its own sake—or confining feeling-attention to the image, within and of itself (like a tapestry without a "weaver's exit").

Any image (or even any thought or any perception), in and of itself, is merely a kind of maze, or a "room" without an exit, or a mode of entrapment in and by "point of view" (or ego's "I").

Rather than being an end in itself, the any image I make and do is an aesthetically fabricated means for participatory ecstasy—wherein and whereby the any rightly participating viewer tacitly transcends "point of view" (or the otherwise inescapable "room" of egoity) by means of participation in Reality Itself.

11.

The image-art I make and do is about entering (or transferring) into the intrinsically egoless Transcendental Sphere and State of Reality Itself.

That process always begins in the sphere of conditionality and superficiality—with the "subjects" of moment to moment attention.

Fully participating in the image-art I make and do requires the viewer to deal with—and go beyond—the "subject-self" (or ego-"self", or "point-of-view-self").

Therefore, fullest right participation in the image-art I make and do is, itself, a profound form of "self"-discipline.

12.

Whatever people look at, they see a reflection of themselves.

Whatever people look at, they manifest themselves in response.

Whatever people look at, they show their own shape in response.

Whatever people look at, they feel their own shape in response.

Therefore, an intrinsic discipline of the habits of egoity—and of "point of view" itself—is required in order to rightly, fully, and fruitfully participate in the image-art I make and do.

Open-Handed Image-Art

It is significant that among the earliest art-forms human beings ever made are images of open hands. The artist would apparently put a hand up against a cave wall and blow contrasting materials out of the mouth (thus creating a silhouette of the hand), or (otherwise) immerse the hand in a contrasting material and press the hand on the wall (thus leaving an impression of the hand).

Such images of open hands are among the oldest art that still exists. And, indeed, the quality of open-handedness—in the sense of freedom from the "self"-contraction of egoic existence—does, in fact, have something to do with why people in prehistoric times would blow contrasting material around their hands or put hand-impressions on cave walls, and with why anybody might do so now.

The breath and the hand—that happening-conjunction says something about what right and true art is.

Right and true art is an open-handedness—not a closed fist, not a dissociated or "self"-contracted gesture.

Right and true art flows to the viewer—rather than being at war with the viewer, or aggressively trying to control and defeat the viewer.

Altogether, right and true art enables and serves the viewer—in an open-handed, ego-transcending manner.

Right and true art is infinitely generous.

Perfect Abstraction

1.

Any and every apparently three-dimensional form of visual experience is—in the immediate instant of any apparent moment of specific experiential observation—intrinsically and self-evidently a <u>two</u>-dimensional (or flat-field) mode of image-experience.

In any specific observational instant, the visual phenomenon is, intrinsically and self-evidently, a timeless, non-changing, flat-field-appearance of juxtaposed elements (such as colors, shapes, and lines), and, altogether, a depthless flat space (or image) of mutually opposing or, otherwise, mutually supportive visual signs (or observables).

No matter how intensively (or for how long a period of time) anyone may walk around or within an apparently three-dimensional form, that walk-around or walk-within is—in the immediate instant of any apparent moment of visual observation in the walking-time of the process—a moment of mere <u>image</u> (or flat-field experience).

Mere image is inherently egoless, flat-patterned, non-familiar, abstract, and unique.

Mere image is never totally comprehensive, or inclusive of all possible views in space, time, or space-time.

Every mere-image instant points beyond itself to an existential totality that cannot be comprehensively and finally experienced or "known".

PERFECT ABSTRACTION

Likewise, every mere-image instant points beyond itself to the egoless, Indivisible, all-and-All-Inclusive, and all-and-All-Transcending Self-Nature, Self-Condition, and Self-State That Is Reality Itself.

2.

All perception is abstraction.

All that is experienced by or from a "point of view" in space, or time, or space-time is non-totality, a selection, a partial view, a mere fraction of the whole.

Every perception experienced by or from a "point of view" is an egoic, or "self"-referring, fabrication.

Right and true visual art, or image-art, must render the "point-of-view"-made and intrinsically ego-bound fabrications that comprise ordinary perception back to the whole of totality.

Right and true visual art, or image-art, must render the "point-of-view"-made and intrinsically ego-bound abstractions that comprise ordinary perception back to the egoless Reality-Source in which perception is otherwise ego-bound.

Right and true visual art, or image-art, is the ego-transcending process of Perfect Abstraction. ■

GLOSSARY

aesthetic ecstasy—Adi Da Samraj uses the word "ecstasy" to mean literally "standing (-*stasis*) outside (*ec-*)" of the separate "point of view", or ego. Thus, aesthetic ecstasy is the process, or moment, of transcending the egoic perspective in the context of participating in true art.

all-and-All—A phrase Adi Da Samraj has created to describe the totality of conditional (or ordinarily appearing) existence—both as the "sum of its parts" and as an undivided whole. He defines lower-case "all" as indicating "the collected sum of all presumed-to-be-separate beings, things, and conditions", and upper-case "All" as indicating "the All (or the undivided totality) of conditional existence as a whole".

anegoic—Literally meaning "non-egoic", Adi Da Samraj uses this term to mean "egoless", or "without the presumption of a separate 'point of view'".

aperspectival—Literally meaning "non-perspectival" (or "not constructed in accordance with the established laws of perspective"), Adi Da Samraj also gives this term the extended meaning of "not constructed so as to support the presumption of a separate 'point of view'".

closed fist / opened hand—Adi Da Samraj has long used the closed fist as a metaphor for the activity of the ego (contracting from the field of relations into a separate "point of view"), and the open hand as a sign of the human being in free and participatory relationship to all it encounters.

conditionality—*See* **Reality Itself**

depth / in-depth—In this book, Adi Da Samraj often uses "depth" or "in-depth" to indicate the domain of human awareness and experience that lies "underneath" or "beyond" conventional, superficial, or social exchanges. Ultimately, the true "in-depth" dimension is Reality Itself.

ego / ego-"I"—Adi Da Samraj defines "ego" not as any kind of personal or psychological entity or essence, but, rather, as an <u>activity</u>—the habitual activity of contraction as a separate "self". The largely unconscious activity of "self"-contraction is the expression of the underlying presumption that "I am separate from everything and everyone else".

As a synonym for "ego", Adi Da Samraj often uses the compound term "ego-'I'". The quotation marks around "I" indicate that, in Reality, there is no such thing as the separate "I", even though it appears to be the case in ordinary experience.

To be "egoless" is to exist entirely without the presumption of separation from Reality Itself, or from anything that appears.

ego-art—*See* **Reality-art**

God-art—*See* **Reality-art**

Non-conditional—Not dependent on "conditions". *See* **Reality Itself**

"object"—Adi Da Samraj consistently places the words "object", "objective", and so forth, in quotation marks. He does this in order to indicate that, in Reality Itself, there is no such thing as an "object" that is separate from the "subject".

Glossary

performance-assisted "subjective" process—A phrase Adi Da Samraj uses for the process of participation in his art and his theatrical works, which indicates that each individual goes through his or her own inward (or "subjective") course of response to the "performance" (or artwork) presented. The "performance" (or artwork) is not intended to be an "objectified" thing, but rather an assistance to a transformation of consciousness for the participant.

"point of view"—By placing this phrase in quotation marks, Adi Da Samraj is communicating that, in Reality, every "point of view" is an illusion—because all ordinary viewpoints are founded in the presumption of the separate existence of "I".

"radical"—Adi Da Samraj uses this word with its core meaning of "at the root", rather than in reference to an extreme (often political) viewpoint.

Reality Itself—Adi Da Samraj distinguishes between two meanings of the word "reality". (1) He refers to reality as we ordinarily perceive it and participate in it as "conditionally manifested reality" (or "conditionality"). This "ordinary reality" is the complex effect of all kinds of causes. Thus, the "ordinary reality" can manifest only in accordance with whatever conditions are the case. Therefore, because the "ordinary reality" is dependent on conditions, Adi Da Samraj describes it as "conditionality". (2) In contrast to ordinary reality, Adi Da Samraj refers to "Reality Itself" (with capital letters). Reality Itself is not, in any sense, dependent on conditions. In other words, Reality Itself is utterly "<u>Non</u>-conditional". Adi Da Samraj states that Reality Itself is the "One and Only Self-Nature, Self-Condition, and Self-State" of every thing and every being in the universe.

PERFECT ABSTRACTION

Reality-art—In his essay "The Maze of Ecstasy", Adi Da Samraj summarizes three phases of art history: The pre-Renaissance focus of art on ideas and myths about "God" (or "God-art"), the post-Renaissance shift to art being an expression of the individual's own "point of view" (or "ego-art"), and his establishment of an art that transcends "point of view" and Reveals Reality Itself ("Reality-art").

"self"—Adi Da Samraj places this term in quotation marks to indicate that the presumption of a concrete separate "self" is an illusion—generated in response to the fact of bodily existence.

"self"-contraction—Adi Da Samraj's descriptive phrase for the ego as the activity of assuming a separate "point of view".

"self"-discipline—With this term, Adi Da Samraj is pointing out that to truly participate in egoless art, one must "discipline" (or, truly, be drawn to transcend) the "point of view" of the ego-"self".

Self-Nature, Self-Condition, and Self-State of Reality Itself—While pointing out that the presumption of an existent separate "self" is an illusion, Adi Da Samraj uses this phrase to describe the True "Self" of everything that appears. Reality Itself is the Substance, Context, and Perfect Truth of existence.

space-time-"located" / "location" / "locatedness"—Adi Da Samraj uses the word "locate" (and variants) to indicate the apparent "location" of any particular ego at a particular point in space. Since the existence of the individual egoic viewpoint is actually a presumption, and not true to Reality Itself, he places the word in quotation marks.

Glossary

"subject"—Adi Da Samraj consistently places the lower-case words "subject", "subjective", and so forth, in quotation marks. He does this in order to indicate that, in Reality Itself, there is no such thing as a "subject" that is separate from all potential "objects".

Transcendental Realism / Realist—In this phrase, Adi Da Samraj uses the word "Realism" or "Realist" (with a capital "R") in a very particular sense. He is not referring to art in which the "subject" is depicted in a conventionally realistic manner. Rather, he is referring to art that communicates the coincidence of the conditional "subject" with Non-conditional (or Transcendental) Reality.

TRANSCENDENTAL REALISM

The Image-Art of egoless Coincidence With Reality Itself

by Adi Da Samraj

Adi Da's writings on the tradition and purpose of true art, and on the profound artistic, philosophical, and revelatory elements of his own image-art. A collection of thirteen essays written to appear in conjunction with the collateral exhibition of Adi Da's art at the 2007 Biennale di Venezia.

More than a verbal explanation of what his art is "really" all about, this body of words, much like Adi Da's art itself, is a "transformational environment". If you have seen Adi Da's art, and wonder what or who it was that moved you, a careful consideration of this text will serve to integrate the immediacy of the aesthetic experience into a transformed understanding—of Adi Da's art, of art altogether, and of the most profound dimensions of human experience.

—from the introduction

Clearly, Adi Da Samraj is creating a new sacred art—and, one might add, one not bound to any particular religious ideology....

It is Adi Da Samraj's imaginative triumph to have conveyed the illusions created by discrepant points of view and the emotionally liberating effect when they aesthetically unite in the psyche of the shocked perceiver.

—**DONALD KUSPIT**
Distinguished art critic; poet; author;
Professor of Art History and Philosophy,
State University of New York, Stony Brook

104 pp., plus 8-page color insert of Adi Da's images, **$19.95**

AESTHETIC ECSTASY

New Essays Written for
Transcendental Realism: The Image-Art of egoless Coincidence with Reality Itself

by Adi Da Samraj

In these new writings from 2007, Adi Da discusses the limits of viewing art via the analytical mind, and describes how to participate fully in his image-art. Adi Da also addresses the culture in which art arises, and calls for a restored understanding of the "human need for beauty" and the retrieval of truly sacred art and culture.

Ecstasy is the primary and fundamental human motive and event. The transcending of "objectification"—whether of "self" or "world" or Reality Itself—is the primary and fundamental characteristic of right and true human purpose. Therefore, the primary and fundamental purpose of right and true art is aesthetic ecstasy—wherein and whereby the human being is served toward the primary and fundamental human purpose and event that is ecstasy itself (or egoless participation in Reality Itself).

—Adi Da Samraj

56 pp., **$6.95**

THE WORLD AS LIGHT

An Introduction to the Art of Adi Da Samraj

by Mei-Ling Israel

The condition of non-separateness—as the true nature of the human situation, and the true nature of Reality altogether—is the core of Adi Da's communication in his art. This generously illustrated book provides an overview of the massive body of highly distinctive artwork Adi Da Samraj has created over the past forty years—accompanied by key statements he has made on his own art and on the artistic process in general. Published on the occasion of Adi Da's collateral exhibition at the 52nd Biennale di Venezia (2007).

> *The living body always wants (with wanting need)*
> *to allow the Light of Perfect Reality into the "room".*
> *Assisting human beings to fulfill that impulse*
> *is what I work to do by every act of image-art.*
> —Adi Da Samraj

Adi Da Samraj's two- and three-dimensional shapes are always concrete communicative realities, statements of a mental order that is never repressive or closed off, but always germinating and unpredictable. In all instances, shapes germinate and multiply with sudden offshoots that reveal the potential of a new geometric eroticism.

—**ACHILLE BONITO OLIVA**
Acclaimed critic; curator; lecturer on contemporary art;
Former Director of two Biennale di Venezia;
Recipient of the Valentino d'Oro, 1991

128 pp., with over 140 color and black-and-white illustrations, **$24.95**

To order
books, tapes, CDs, DVDs, and videos
by and about Adi Da Samraj,
contact the Dawn Horse Press:

1-877-770-0772 (from within North America)

1-707-928-6653 (from outside North America)

Or visit the Dawn Horse Press website:

www.dawnhorsepress.com

THE ART OF ADI DA SAMRAJ

TRANSCENDENTAL REALISM:
The Art of Adi Da Samraj
Catalogue of the Collateral Exhibition
at the 2007 Venice Biennale

THE SPECTRA SUITES
by Adi Da Samraj

THE QUANDRA LOKA SUITE: 52 VIEWS
by Adi Da Samraj

THE BRIGHT FIELD:
The Photographic Art of Samraj Adi Da

For more information on the art of Adi Da Samraj,
or to order the above books and catalogues,
please contact:

www.daplastique.com
info@daplastique.com